INSPIRING ARTISTS

PIETER BRUEGEL THE ELDER

Published in 2016 by The Rosen Publishing Group, Inc.
29 East 21st Street, New York, NY 10010

First Edition

Library of Congress Cataloging-in-Publication Data

Rockett, Paul.
Pieter Bruegel the Elder/ Paul Rockett.
pages cm. -- (Inspiring artists)
Includes index.
ISBN 978-1-5081-7060-0 (library bound)
1. Bruegel, Pieter, approximately 1525-1569--Juvenile literature. 2. Painters--Belgium--Biography--Juvenile literature. I. Title.
ND673.B73R627 2015
759.9493--dc23
2015023353

Manufactured in the United States of America

INSPIRING ARTISTS
PIETER BRUEGEL THE ELDER

Paul Rockett

ROSEN
PUBLISHING®
New York

Every attempt has been made to clear copyright. Should there be any inadvertent omission please apply to the publisher for rectification.

CONTENTS

Man of mystery

Pieter Bruegel is now famous as a painter of sweeping landscapes and rowdy peasant life, but he first became known for his print designs. Many of his pictures are puzzling; some are humorous, others horrifying. He was born in the Netherlands probably between 1525 and 1530, and he died young in 1569. He left no written record about his life or work, and there are no contemporary biographies, so we know very little about him.

"Bruegel was a very quiet and thoughtful man, not fond of talking, but ready with jokes when in the company of others. He liked to frighten people ... with all kinds of spooks and uncanny noises."
– Karel van Mander, art historian, 1604

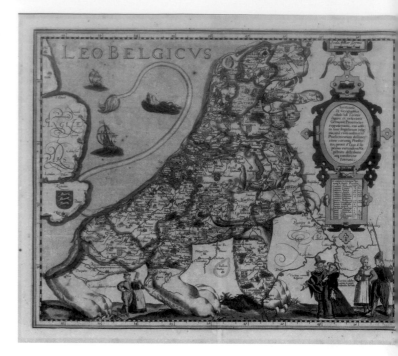

A 16th century map of the Netherland and the Low Countries, drawn to form the shape of a lion.

Birthplace

We do not know exactly where in the Netherlands Bruegel was born. In his lifetime, the Netherlands was part of an area known as the Low Countries. These were made up of 17 provinces along the coast of the North Sea, bordering Germany. They included present-day Belgium, Holland and Luxembourg.

Religious unrest

Some years before Bruegel's birth, the German monk Martin Luther (1483–1546) published a series of complaints about the Catholic Church. Soon, many people in different countries joined what came to be called the Protestant Reformation. From 1555 the Spanish Catholic ruler of the Netherlands, King Philip II, tried to stop the revolts with harsh measures, even sending troops to kill the rebels. Bruegel may have secretly addressed these events in some of his paintings (see *Massacre of the Innocents* on p.35). Violence spread on both sides. A year before Bruegel's death, real war broke out between the Netherlands and Spain. It would rage on for 80 years.

The Painter and the Art Lover, believed to be a self-portrait, 1566

The Procession to Calvary, 1564

Cities and success

Because Bruegel painted country people, it was thought he must have been one, and he is sometimes called "Peasant Bruegel." In fact, he spent most of his life in cities. Netherlandish cities at this time were growing in size and wealth, and were important centers of international trade and banking. It was there that artists found employment. While most painters of his day specialized in portraits, or worked for princely palaces and the Church so that their pictures were visible to the public, Bruegel did none of these things. His patrons were scholars and businessmen, collectors who kept their pictures at home. He spent many years employed making drawings for prints, which were widely known, but his paintings only became popular after his death. Over the centuries, they have inspired artists, writers and even filmmakers.

A still from the 2011 film *The Mill and the Cross*. The film is based on Bruegel's *The Procession to Calvary* (above).

The journey begins

Bruegel's journey as an artist began in the city of Brussels, where he may have been apprenticed to one of the most successful painters of the Low Countries, Pieter Coecke van Aelst (1502–1550). Bruegel later married van Aelst's daughter.

Italian inspiration

Van Aelst was a versatile artist who painted portraits and religious scenes and designed stained glass windows and tapestries for the Spanish court. Like most ambitious 16th century northern European artists, van Aelst had travelled to Italy and was influenced by Italian Renaissance painters. It may have been van Aelst who prompted Bruegel to visit Italy himself. After being admitted as an independent master to the Antwerp Painters' Guild in 1551, Bruegel headed off on his own Italian adventure.

Crossing the Alps

Rather than looking at the work of foreign artists on his travels, Bruegel recorded the landscape through which he travelled. Coming from the flat, coastal Low Countries, he was fascinated by mountain scenery. While crossing the Alps, Bruegel made sketches that he would use in his work for the rest of his life.

> *"...while he visited the Alps, Bruegel had swallowed all the mountains and cliffs, and upon coming home, he spat them out upon his canvases and panels..."*
> – Karel van Mander, art historian, 1604

Alpine Landscape, c.1552

Portrait of Giulio Clovio (pointing to his illuminated manuscript of the Farnese Hours), El Greco, 1571–72

Rome

When he reached Rome, Bruegel made friends with a famous miniaturist, the Croatian-born Giulio Clovio (1498–1578). A miniaturist paints very small, detailed pictures; Clovio specialized in illustrating precious prayer books. A list of Clovio's belongings made after his death mentions a miniature painted half by him and half by Bruegel. The Netherlandish artist continued to insert tiny details into his paintings all his life.

Large landscapes

In about 1555 Bruegel returned to Antwerp, once again crossing the Alps, where he made many sketches, including *Solicitudo Rustica* (left) that formed the basis of a series of 12 etchings of large landscapes. These were his first commercial success, thanks to the invention of the printing press. These prints were also important models for his series of paintings of the changing seasons (see p.28–33).

Solicitudo Rustica, 1555

The power of print

In 1556 Bruegel went to work for the Antwerp printer and publisher Hieronymus Cock (1518–1570), making drawings that would be engraved or etched by others.

The printing press

At this time printing was a big, money-making, business. The printing press had been around for just over a hundred years and meant that printed pamphlets, and later books, could be circulated widely across Europe. Printers also made prints of artworks that reached a much wider audience than a painting could.

This print is from the 16th century and shows the inside of a printing press house.

Steady money

Bruegel earned a steady income by working for Hieronymus Cock. He supplied drawings that were engraved by another person and then printed and sold across the continent. As well as landscapes, printed images of religious and moral subjects were also extremely popular and, Bruegel drew whatever subject was in demand.

Hieronymus Bosch

Prints of works by Dutch artist Hieronymus Bosch (1450s–1516) were extremely popular. Bosch died in 1516, but the continuing demand for his work led many artists, such as Bruegel, to copy his style. Bosch's work contained moral messages from the Bible, presented within imaginary landscapes filled with creatures, that often looked like characters from dreams or nightmares. In his painting *The Garden of Earthly Delights* (top right), Bosch painted three panels showing different landscapes filled with people as well as local and exotic animals and strange beings. The left panel depicts the Garden of Eden, with God bringing Adam and Eve together; the middle panel is the garden of the title, showing people revelling in guilty pleasures; the panel on the right shows a hellish landscape, the place for those who fall under the temptations of evil. The influence of Bosch's style can be seen in many of Bruegel's early prints and some of his paintings. For a while he was known as the "second Bosch."

The Garden of Earthly Delights, Hieronymus Bosch, c.1500

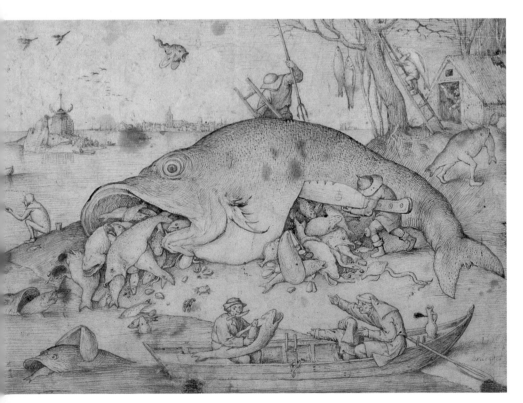

Big Fish Eat Little Fish, c.1556

Big Fish Eat Little Fish

Proverbs were also popular subjects for prints. Proverbs are sayings that convey a commonly believed truth. Bruegel's print design, *Big Fish Eat Little Fish* (left), illustrates this proverb, showing us that the big and powerful swallow up and use those who are smaller and weaker.

Big Fish Eat Little Fish shows similarities to the work of Bosch. Both artists included fantasy elements, seen here as fish with legs and fish flying in the air. The preparatory drawing was done by Bruegel, but the engraving made from it was signed with Bosch's name, possibly to increase sales.

11

Vice and virtue

Between 1555 and 1563 Bruegel supplied Cock with around 40 drawings that were made into prints. His work was celebrated for his comic scenes, and his range of styles, from the fantastical to the realistic.

Vices

In 1556 Bruegel completed a series of seven drawings called *The Vices*. The theme of vice, or the Seven Deadly Sins (lust, gluttony, greed, sloth, anger, envy and pride), was traditional in art, with many examples in medieval sculpture and manuscript illumination. Each drawing in *The Vices* shows a woman acting out a vice in a fantasy land surrounded by monsters that symbolize different aspects of her wickedness. The grotesque images in each print clearly show Bosch's influence.

Virtues

By 1560 Bruegel had completed a companion piece to *The Vices* that showed acts of goodness (faith, hope, charity, temperance, prudence, justice and fortitude), known as *The Virtues*. In each, a woman is placed within a familiar setting and there are no monsters; her actions are grounded in reality. These prints show Bruegel developing his own style based on real observation rather than the fantastical style influenced by Bosch.

Gluttony, 1556

Charity, 1560

The Fat Kitchen, 1563

The Thin Kitchen, 1563

Satire and social criticism

Many of Bruegel's prints are celebrated for their use of satire, a form of social commentary that uses to correct vice and instill virtue. This was a strong feature of Bosch's art. Bruegel's satire does this through grotesque caricatures, creating images that would go on to influence future political cartoonists.

In *The Fat Kitchen* Bruegel exaggerates the shape and behavior of people who are greedy. Note how the greedy man is pushing a starving beggar away from the door. *The Thin Kitchen* critiques those who live in self-denial, making both groups of people look foolish. These contrasting images are used by the 19th century British satirist James Gillray (1756–1815) in his illustration *French Liberty, British Slavery*. Here, the two exaggerated body shapes are used to criticize the different governments of France and Britain.

Art

Both The Fat Kitchen *and* The Thin Kitchen *prints (above) show similar actions taking place as people sit down to eat. What elements in each print emphasise one group as being greedy and the other as being frugal?*

French Liberty, British Slavery, James Gillray, 1792

World landscapes

While Bruegel made a name for himself as a print designer, he was also working away at large-scale paintings. These were vast, technicolor visions of the natural world that showed the skills he had developed in his landscape drawings. They also revealed the influence of a painting style known as "world landscape."

God's eye view

Netherlandish painter Joachim Patinir (c.1480–1524) is believed to be the first artist to develop a style of composition known as world landscape. His aim was to give the impression that the whole world could fit within one painting. This meant that lots of different natural features, such as mountains, forests and the sea were shown, as seen below in Patinir's painting of Saint Jerome living as a hermit in the Syrian desert. The landscape is also shown from a high viewpoint, as if the viewer were God looking down upon his creation.

Bruegel's world view

World landscape paintings had a huge impact on Bruegel. He developed the style further by adding much greater detail to the depictions of wildlife. He also introduced more familiar scenes of villages and farms from his present-day Netherlands and moved away from depicting only religious scenes.

Saint Jerome in the Desert, Joachim Patinir, c.1520

Mountain high, country low

Many of Bruegel's landscapes are invented combinations of scenery that he recorded on his travels. In *Landscape with Flight into Egypt* (right), Bruegel sets Jesus, Mary, and Joseph's flight from persecution in a European landscape. To add contrast and variety to the scene, Bruegel has grafted in sections of the Alps alongside forests, fields and villages from the Netherlands.

Landscape with Flight into Egypt, 1563

Art

What do you think Lowry's and Bruegel's landscapes tell us about the time in which they were painted?

L.S. Lowry

Twentieth century painter, L.S. Lowry (1887–1976) developed a style of world landscape compositions that show a very different world to Bruegel's. Both Bruegel and Lowry used a high viewpoint, but where Bruegel shows the natural world, Lowry's pictures show a vast stretch of an industrial landscape, where factories and chimneys tower in place of trees and mountains. Both artists show human life as dominated by the landscape: In Bruegel the life of people is tied to nature and the seasons, whereas for Lowry the figures are products of the factories, and appear less real than the buildings that surround them.

The Pond, L. S. Lowry, 1950

The Fall of Icarus

Towards the end of the 1550s Bruegel's landscape paintings began to focus more on the behavior of ordinary people. This can be seen in his painting *The Fall of Icarus*, which is based on a famous Greek myth. Bruegel adds a twist to this tale, placing more importance on the detail of everyday peasant life than on the actions of a tragic hero.

An unimportant failure

Icarus' father, Daedalus, was a craftsman who had been imprisoned in the labyrinth on the island of Crete along with his son. Daedalus made two pairs of wings and gave one pair to Icarus, warning him not to fly too close to the hot sun. Icarus did not heed the warning and his wings melted, causing him to fall into the sea and drown. In the painting, the character of Icarus only appears as a small detail—just as a pair of legs. The main figure is a farmer pushing his plough, and refers to a Netherlandish proverb: "No plough stops because a man dies." Like the other people in the painting, the farmer is too busy with his own life to show any interest in the fall of Icarus.

Icarus' legs can be seen disappearing into the sea in this detail from The Fall of Icarus *(below).*

The Fall of Icarus, c.1558

The Fall of Icarus, Rubens, 1636

Icarus paintings

The story of Icarus has inspired many painters, from as far back as 100 BCE to the 20th century. However, they all make the character of Icarus much more central. In Dutch artist Peter Paul Rubens' (1577–1640) sketch (above) Icarus is shown at the most dramatic point in the story, as he falls helpless through the sky. His body takes up the central space of the composition. His movement and the worried gaze of Daedalus also direct our attention towards him. In comparison, Bruegel's approach to the story is more unusual and original.

Inspiring poetry

Bruegel's paintings have gone on to inspire writers as well as visual artists. American poet, William Carlos Williams (1883–1963), published a whole book of poetry based on Bruegel's paintings. The poet, W. H. Auden (1907–1973) wrote a famous poem around Bruegel's *The Fall of Icarus*, called "Musée des Beaux Arts." It describes Icarus' fall as an "unimportant failure," noting how Bruegel understood that some events are not important to everyone.

Disputed work

Some experts think that *The Fall of Icarus* is not by Bruegel, but may be a copy of a lost original that was made by one of his followers. They have pointed out the lack of detail in the background and suggested that the poses of the horse and peasant appear awkward and not that well executed, unlike Bruegel's other work.

Painted puzzles

Up until 1559 Bruegel had been signing his work as "Brueghel," but for some reason he decided to drop the "h." This change was made in a year when he embarked on a series of ambitious new paintings that showed a move away from natural landscapes and towards landscapes of human behavior.

Proverb country

Proverbs are short, familiar sayings that are often used to deliver a moral message. They were made popular in the Netherlands by the influential scholar Desiderius Erasmus (1466–1536). In 1500, Erasmus published a collection of thousands of different proverbs from all over Europe. These included many that are still used today, such as "to leave no stone unturned" and "to break the ice."

Netherlandish Proverbs, 1559

Unusual actions

Bruegel's painting *Netherlandish Proverbs* contains over 100 different proverbs. Proverbs often describe unusual actions to express their meaning and in illustrating them word for word Bruegel shows a village full of people behaving very oddly. These unusual actions act as a puzzle for the viewer to try and work out which proverbs they're designed to show.

This figure illustrates the proverbs, "To bang your head against a brick wall," which means to try and achieve something impossible, and "One foot shod, the other one bare," meaning balance is everything.

Frans Hogenberg

A year before Bruegel completed his painting, Frans Hogenberg (1535–1590) produced a print called *The Blue Hood*, which was filled with people acting out different proverbs. Hosenberg was a painter, engraver and mapmaker, who like Bruegel, had worked for the printing house of Hieronymus Cock. It was common at this time for artists to copy each other's designs, making small changes. Bruegel has clearly been inspired by Hogenberg's print, keeping some of the same proverbs, but moving the action into a village.

The Blue Hood, Frans Hogenberg, 1558

Inspired update

The 20th century US artist Thomas E. Breitenbach (1951–) used proverbs as the theme of his *Proverbidioms* (below), which contains over 300 different sayings. These include the proverb "You are what you eat," shown by a giant carrot eating a small carrot, and the idiom "to hit the sack," shown by the man on the balcony hitting a sack.

Proverbidioms, Thomas E. Breitenbach, 1975

Art How do the images seen in the section of *Proverbidioms* below pay tribute to Bruegel? What significance does the crossed out "h" and the number "1559" have?

Encyclopedic illustrators

The *Netherlandish Proverbs* form part of a small group of paintings by Bruegel that are sometimes referred to as his "encyclopedia paintings" as they each contain a huge amount of information. These paintings appear as visual puzzles and have inspired many children's illustrators, such as Richard Scarry and Martin Handford, creator of *Where's Waldo?* books.

Children's Games

Bruegel's paintings are so full of detail that they are often used as a historical reference to life in the 16th century. They show us glimpses of the lives of people that were not usually shown in paintings, such as the poor and children. Bruegel's *Children's Games*, with its depiction of some 230 children, tells us what kinds of games children used to play.

Games

This painting shows over 80 different games. By studying it we can find out which games have remained popular 400 years later and those that are now no longer played. Games like leapfrog and marbles may be instantly recognizable; knucklebones (throwing bones into the air to catch), is a variation on the game of jacks; while barrel-riding is no longer seen.

A hidden message?

At first glance this painting looks like it has been painted to celebrate children at play, but it can also be interpreted as something more meaningful. The action takes place in front of the town hall, the seat of government. Perhaps Bruegel is criticising the way adults run the town, comparing their behavior to that of children.

Complex compositions

Although the scene shows playful chaos, the composition is in fact carefully ordered. The children fall into a loose series of rows that comes down from the furthest point in the top right (see opposite). The painting is divided into three vertical panels, with the town hall at the top of the central column. These invisible lines help guide our eyes around the painting.

Children's Games, 1560

Art

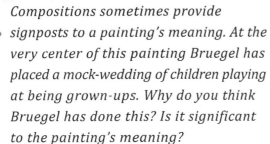

Compositions sometimes provide signposts to a painting's meaning. At the very center of this painting Bruegel has placed a mock-wedding of children playing at being grown-ups. Why do you think Bruegel has done this? Is it significant to the painting's meaning?

James Ensor

Like Bruegel's *Children's Games*, the artworks by James Ensor (1860–1949) may not always be about what they first appear. Ensor was influenced by Bruegel's depictions of busy, playful scenes and uses them to hide criticisms of the world around him. In his drawing, *White and Red Clowns Evolving* (left), the clowns represent mankind. In the background are buildings that suggest a civilized world, and yet it is lived in by clowns. Like *Children's Games*, this image shows us a world in which responsible adults are absent and no one is in control. Ensor's work often criticizes religious and political institutions, as well as people who blindly choose to accept what they are told; for him, these people are no better than clowns.

White and Red Clowns Evolving, James Ensor, 1890

Surreal beings

In 1562 Bruegel created a small group of paintings that stand out from the rest of his work through their images of nightmarish horror. These paintings show Bruegel at his most fantastical, creating monsters that would inspire future artists to unleash their own strange demons.

Mad Meg

Bruegel's 1562 painting *Dulle Griet (Mad Meg)* (below) was inspired by the story of a woman who tricked Hell and stole its valuables. Meg strides forth across a scene that glows like a volcano erupting, while demons are being fought by an army of women.

This painting shows the influence of Hieronymus Bosch more than any other. It also shows elements that are more Bruegel than Bosch, for example a raised foreground is used to create a focus point for the main character. This is a composition that Bruegel uses in a lot of his work.

Fall of the Rebel Angels, Frans Floris, 1554

The Fall of the Rebel Angels

Another Bruegel painting from 1562 is *The Fall of the Rebel Angels* (opposite, top). This depicts a passage from the Bible's Book of Revelations (Chapter 12, verses 2-9), in which a group of angels have rebelled against God and are being thrown out of Heaven by the good angels. Frans Floris (1517–1570) painted this subject eight years earlier (above) and Bruegel would probably have seen Floris' version. Bruegel may have been inspired to copy Floris' composition, showing a squashed mass of monsters at the bottom of the painting. However, their

Dulle Griet (Mad Meg), 1562

The Fall of the Rebel Angels, 1562

monsters show different influences. Floris' monsters are beasts from classical mythology. Bruegel's creatures are nightmarish mixtures of animals, humans and even vegetables.

Surrealism

The Surrealist art movement aimed to find ways to represent dreams, nightmares and the unconscious mind. The creatures in Bruegel's paintings inspired Surrealist artists, such as Leonora Carrington (1917–2011), who saw them as presenting a clash between a real and an imagined world. Carrington's works are filled with personal symbolism.

The background of *Ulu's Pants* (below) shows a stately garden that recalls Carrington's wealthy upbringing, while the monsters contain fragments of folktales and of the artist's own imagination.

Ulu's Pants, Leonora Carrington, 1952

The *Triumph of Death*

Bruegel's most terrifying painting of 1562 is the *Triumph of Death*. It follows a tradition of artwork that shows the figure of Death as a skeleton leading people to their grave. Bruegel's painting shows a scene of mass extinction, with Death and a skeleton army killing everything in sight, making reference to a large plague that killed millions in Europe alone.

Killer disease

The Black Death was a deadly plague transmitted by bacteria carried by fleas that lived on rats. It first spread to Europe from Asia in 1348, killing about a third of the population. It then recurred many times in different forms until the nineteenth century. Bruegel lived through two outbreaks, in 1544–1548 and 1563–1566.

The death theme

The Black Death led to a new theme in Italian art, also known as the "Triumph of Death."

Triumph of Death, artist unknown, c.1448

Plagues were commemorated by showing Death as a skeleton riding a horse above people who were soon to die. Bruegel would have seen the anonymous painting (above) on his travels through Italy and reproduced the image at the very center of his painting.

Triumph of Death, 1562

Danse Macabre, Guyot Marchant, 1485

A deadly tradition

Bruegel's *Triumph of Death* may also have been inspired by northern European imagery of skeletons leading people off to their graves. The original Dance of Death is believed to have been painted on a Paris cemetery wall in 1424, and was published in woodcuts by printer Guyot Marchant in 1485 (above). Here you can see skeletons, representing death, leading a holy man and a constable away.

Rich and poor

In the 16th century, German artist Hans Holbein the Younger (1497–1543) created a popular series of prints that showed Death gathering people from all social backgrounds, rich and poor, old and young. This highlighted the universal nature of death, something that Bruegel also represents, with both royalty and peasants suffering in his painting. It also reinforced the message that we should live a good life, since death comes to all of us, often without warning.

Death and the Mendicant Friar, from *"The Dance of Death,"* Hans Holbein the Younger, c.1538,

Towers of Babel

By the end of 1562 Bruegel had left Antwerp. The city had become overcrowded and filled with new building projects; the population had nearly doubled in size in 50 years. Bruegel's reflections on Antwerp can be seen in his next great paintings of the Tower of Babel.

What was the Tower of Babel?

Bruegel's *Tower of Babel* paintings recount a story from the Bible in which the people of Babylon begin building a tower with the aim that it should reach high up into the heavens (Genesis, Chapter 11, verses 4–9). God is unhappy with this plan, seeing the people as being greedy, ambitious and turning away from religion. He intervenes, mixing up the people's language so that they can no longer understand each other and causing the tower to crumble.

Antwerp: a modern Babel

Bruegel sets his towers in the city of Antwerp as it appeared when he lived there. Antwerp was filled with languages spoken from all over Europe; it was becoming one of the most important commercial centers on the continent. By setting his tower here, Bruegel may be portraying Antwerp as a new Babel.

Art *To the bottom right of the tower in the 1563 painting is a large castle. On the tower's different levels are cottages for the labourers. How does the inclusion of these buildings and their positions help emphasise the scale of the tower?*

Tower of Babel, 1563

Tower of Babel, 1564

Details

Bruegel painted three versions of the *Tower of Babel*, one in 1563, one in 1564 and an earlier version, now lost, that he made in Rome. This version was believed to have been a miniature painting. Bruegel's skill as a miniaturist painter can be seen in the small details of the surviving paintings, which accurately show 16th century building techniques.

The builders are using a system of winches and pulleys and a treadwheel crane to lift the stones for the Tower.

Inspiring Babel buildings

The Colosseum in Rome was the inspiration for Bruegel's towers. His design became the standard image of the Towers of Babel that have appeared in paintings and prints since. Some people even think that the European Union Parliament building may have been based on Bruegel's design.

The Colosseum in Rome, Italy, was completed in 80 CE.

Months (1)

In 1563 Bruegel moved to Brussels, where he married van Aelst's daughter (her name is not known for sure). A year later they had their first child. Around this time Bruegel began reducing his print work and began producing many more paintings. This was a sign of his success amongst art collectors, encouraging him to work on paintings of greater scale and ambition.

Commissions

Little is known about the people who commissioned Bruegel's paintings, with the exception of the wealthy banker Nicolaes Jonghelinck (1530–1606). In 1565 he commissioned Bruegel to produce his most ambitious paintings so far—a series dedicated to the months of the year. Jonghelinck commissioned the *Months* series to hang on his dining room wall. Here they would have been shown off to wealthy visitors, showing them a world beyond their city lives. Six paintings were completed, one for every two months of the year, of which only five have survived.

The Month of October: Ploughing and Sowing, from a *Book of Hours,* anonymous, 1490

Book of Hours

The subject of the *Months* came from illustrations that appeared in medieval manuscripts, such as a Book of Hours (above). These religious books contained a selection of Bible verses, hymns and prayers, as well as a calendar of religious festivals. Sometimes the calendars were accompanied by small illustrations showing the kind of work or activities common to each month of the year.

The Gloomy Day, 1565 (believed to show February and March)

The Return of the Herd, 1565 (believed to show October and November)

While this subject was not new, Bruegel broke new ground by reimagining it in large paintings, and in doing so transformed it into a respected art form.

Man and nature

Each painting of the *Months* shows work and play as shaped by the different season. Bruegel uses lines within his compositions to connect man closely to the landscape. His figures form part of the curves and diagonal lines that move from the foreground into the distance. In *The Return of the Herd* (above) workers are bringing cattle to their winter home. They are just as much a part of the natural environment as the river is, both forming the zigzag line that pulls us into the landscape.

The Harvesters, 1565 (believed to show July and August)

Future inspiration

As Bruegel's paintings were made for private owners, for a long time the public did not get to see them. However, towards the end of the 16th century the *Months* were bought by the City of Antwerp and were put on public display. The paintings were highly praised and created a trend for paintings of landscapes that showed peasants living alongside nature (see p.30–31).

Months (II)

The paintings of the *Months* show a triumphant coming together of Bruegel's awe-inspiring landscapes, his attention to detail and his cast of village characters. While the paintings beautifully capture the atmosphere of each season, they also place a focus on what would become a major new subject in art: scenes of everyday life.

Haymaking, 1565 (believed to show June and July)

Genre painting

Bruegel's focus on people at work and at play led to a style of artwork known as "genre painting." Working people, who could never afford to buy artwork, were now made its central subject. Many of these paintings showed romantic and idealised images of the poor, leading happy and simple lives. However, as genre painting developed, artists began to show images of the poor struggling with their lives and work.

Return from the Harvest, Rubens, 1635

Happy workers

The influence of the *Months* can be seen in the rural scenes painted by Rubens (see also p.17). Rubens was a great admirer of Bruegel, and his painting *Return from the Harvest* (below) copies the subject and elements of composition from Bruegel's *Haymaking* (above), produced 70 years earlier. Both paintings show happy peasants strolling home from a day's work in an open stretch of road that fills the foreground.

The Gleaners, Jean-François Millet, 1857

They express an ideal of man working in harmony with nature, where everything proceeds under the watchful eye of God and in unity with the seasons.

Is this real life?

While Bruegel's paintings accurately show the farming and leisure activities of his time, their depictions of men living in harmony with nature are not always that realistic. In 1565, the year the paintings were completed, there had been a particularly bad harvest in the Netherlands, causing many people to go hungry.

Jean-François Millet

Two hundred years after Bruegel's *Months* appeared, French artist Jean-François Millet (1814–1875) became famous for his paintings of peasants struggling with farmwork. Unlike Bruegel's paintings, which were not specific to a particular time or social condition, Millet investigated the very real hard lot of 19th century French farm workers. Instead of the golden fields and happy workforce of Bruegel's *Haymaking*, Millet's painting *The Gleaners* (above) shows a dull-colored scene of women searching for leftover bits of grain.

Art

The viewpoint in The Gleaners *is very different from that depicted in the paintings of the* Months. *How does this alter the way we see the figures in the painting?*

31

Months III: Hunters in the Snow

Hunters in the Snow is considered by many people to be the most impressive painting of the *Months* series. In it, nature is frozen but full of life; the colors provide a winter chill in a composition that carefully plots out both the hardships and rewards of nature's toughest season.

Work and play

Hunters in the Snow is a painting of two halves. The left side shows people at work, be it preparing food or returning from a hunt. The right side shows people playing on the frozen ponds. This split in the painting is emphasised by the vertical lines of the trees on the left contrasting with the horizontal rows across the pond on the right.

Like all of Bruegel's paintings, *Hunters in the Snow* is filled with tiny details, such as the firemen putting out a chimney fire on a house in the distance.

Hunters in the Snow, 1565 (believed to show December and January)

A Hunting Scene, Jeff Wall, 1994

Cold colors

In the *Months* the temperature of each season is felt through the use of color. *Hunters in the Snow* uses a small palette of colors that conjure up the cold feeling of winter. The image is mainly made up of the white of the snow and the pale green in the sky and frozen ponds. Bruegel has used a thin coat of paint (a glaze) on the sky and ice, giving it a translucent icy effect, while the rest of the painting is completed in thicker, impasto layers of paint that allow for more detail.

A Hunting Scene

U.S. artist Jeff Wall (1946–) took his inspiration for the photo *A Hunting Scene* from Bruegel's painting. Both images contain a curve to the left where their hunters stand. But while the majority of Bruegel's image contains landscape, Wall's photo is mainly filled with cold sky. Wall's image is a photographic transparency mounted on a light box. The light box projects white light through the image, adding a cold and colorless glow to the scene. This and other differences make Wall's photo appear more chilling than Bruegel's painting, even though it features no snow.

Art

Both Bruegel and Wall have applied different techniques to create a cold, white winter feel. How do the actions or lack of actions in each image help us to identify the season as winter?'

Hidden in the snow

Bruegel went on to paint many winter scenes after he finished the *Months*. These would become his most popular landscapes. However, the snow in these scenes sometimes contained traps and hid unpleasant truths.

Let it snow

In the same year that Bruegel painted *Hunters in the Snow* he completed *Winter Landscape with Birdtrap* (right). At first glance, this painting seems to celebrate play in wintertime, but the detail of the birdtrap to the right suggests that life is not all fun and games, and that freedom could be taken away at any moment.

Winter Landscape with Birdtrap, 1565

In the 17th century this was Bruegel's most popular painting. Many artists copied it, with around 140 known versions made. Dutch artist Hendrick Avercamp (1585–1634) made a successful career producing variations of the painting. Many of Avercamp's snow scenes have since become popular Christmas card images.

Winter Landscape with Ice Skaters, Hendrick Avercamp, c.1608

The birdtrap is made of an old door propped up on a stick.

Massacre of the Innocents, 1567

Bethlehem in Belgium

Bruegel painted a number of snow scenes in which stories from the Bible take place in a Netherlandish village. One of these paintings, *Massacre of the Innocents* (above), tells the story in the Bible (Gospel of Matthew, Chapter 2, verses 13–23) of when King Herod heard the news of Jesus' birth and ordered that all male babies and young children in Bethlehem be murdered.

Although we don't have any clear knowledge of Bruegel's intentions, the painting can be seen as showing the religious unrest of his own time. In 1567, the year the painting was completed, Philip II of Spain ordered 10,000 soldiers to march into the Netherlands and end a Protestant rebellion. Men, women and children, in villages like the one in the painting, were put to death.

Censorship

Ten years after *Massacre of the Innocents* was completed, it came into the possession of Rudolf II, the Holy Roman Emperor and nephew of Philip II. Rudolf had been raised in the Spanish Catholic court and ordered any details of children being killed to be painted over with images of animals. This act of censorship suggests that whether or not Bruegel had meant there to be a parallel between the Bible story and the Spanish soldiers' brutal actions in 1567, it had come to be read this way.

In this close-up you can just about see the original image of a child that has been painted over with a swan on top of him.

Peasant Bruegel

From 1567 Bruegel became less interested in landscapes and focused more on the lives of peasants, showing them at traditional celebrations and weddings. His ability to take the viewer into their world earned him the nickname "Peasant Bruegel," and also led many to assume that he had lived his early life as a peasant.

Peasant legend

There is a legend that tells of Bruegel dressing up in peasant clothes and going to the weddings and other celebrations of peasants. It is thought that he did this in order to study their lives and behavior close up, and that by surrounding himself by peasant life he was able to represent their world more richly and realistically.

Peasant Wedding

In his painting *Peasant Wedding* (below), Bruegel has abandoned a high viewpoint so that we see the scene on the same level as the people within it. This makes us feel like we are inside the village hall with them, sitting at a neighbouring table at the feast.

 **Art**

Look closely at the clothes and the positions of the people in Peasant Wedding. *What do they tell us about the lives of the people?*

Peasant Wedding, 1567

Sigrid Holmwood

Both Bruegel and artist Sigrid Holmwood (1978–) record peasant customs and celebrations in their work. Bruegel's *Peasant Dance* is also known as *The Village Kermis*, a kermis being a festival that celebrates a local patron saint. Holmswood's painting *Leaping Hogs Acre Boundary Ditch* (right) refers to an Anglo-Saxon tradition called "beating the bounds," where people would beat sticks along the boundary of the village to mark their territory. Holmwood goes one step further by only using techniques and materials that a peasant painter would have had access to, making her paints out of different colored berries, and crushed insects.

Peasant Dance, 1567

Leaping Hogs Acre Boundary Ditch, Sigrid Holmwood, 2008

Figures to the fore

In Bruegel's later work the large bulky forms of peasants dominate the composition and nature moves to the background. His figures show a renewed interest in Italian art and references to prints that were widely circulated at the time.

Sculptural forms

One of the most famous engravings of the 16th century is *The Death of Ananias*, (below) by Italian Agostino Veneziano (c.1490–c.1540) from a drawing made by leading Italian Renaissance artist Raphael (1483–1520). Veneziano worked in Raphael's workshop in Rome. This image was widely distributed and Bruegel would most certainly have seen it.

The print depicts a scene from the Bible when Ananias is struck down dead after lying to Saint Peter about having given up his entire wealth (Gospel of Luke, Acts 5: verses 1–11). The print shows Raphael's interest in strong, solid figures. This quality is emphasised in Veneziano's work, where the gray tones pick out the figure's big, muscular limbs. This three-dimensional aspect can also be seen in the solid and rounded shapes of Bruegel's figures.

Peasant Couple Dancing, Albrecht Dürer, 1514,

Peasant forms

German artist Albrecht Dürer (1471–1528) had also been influenced by figurative Italian art and had travelled to Italy twice, studying classical sculpture. His prints would also have been familiar to Bruegel, and both produced work around peasants dancing. Dürer's *Peasant Couple Dancing* (above) shows sturdy forms that lack the graceful movements of Veneziano's etched figures; they have a weight that suggests a heavy stomp at every footfall, with the lack of background emphasising their sculptural quality. Like the figures in Dürer's print, Bruegel's peasants are also stocky and solid-looking.

The Death of Ananias, Agostino Veneziano (Agostino dei Musi), c.1516

Bruegel's bodies

The prints of Veneziano and Dürer place the figure in the foreground, with their movement and form becoming the center of attention. This becomes part of Bruegel's focus in capturing the behavior of his peasant subjects. In *The Wedding Dance* (below) the movements of the dancers lead us around the painting, while the central sturdy figure in *The Peasant and the Bird-nester* (right) dominates the painting as he strides directly towards us.

The Wedding Dance, 1566

The Peasant and the Bird-nester, 1568

War and death

By 1568 Bruegel's output of paintings had slowed down. The Eighty Years' War had just begun, with the Netherlands fighting for independence from Spanish rule (see p.6). This was a time of great disruption and fear.

The Misanthrope

The final paintings that Bruegel made all reflect a sense of death and darkness. This may be a response to the outbreak of fighting and climate of fear in the Netherlands at that time.

Bruegel's painting *The Misanthrope* (the name for someone who hates mankind) represents a man wanting to leave the world and contains the following caption: "Because the world is so unfaithful, I am going into mourning." However, his pathway offers him no safe directions; on one side he is being robbed and on the other he is about to step on sharp thorns.

Gallows bird

In *The Magpie on the Gallows* (opposite, top), Bruegel's vast landscapes and peasant celebration come together, but the central image is that of a gallows. Gallows are wooden structures from which people were hanged. On top of the gallows sits a magpie, a bird that symbolizes bad luck and also the expression "to babble like a magpie" (which means "to be a gossip").

Some people have read these symbols as representing the fear of expressing political or religious views in Netherlands at this time, and that to say too much might lead to your death.

Art

The robber in The Misanthrope *is encased in a globe that represents the world. This shows the man as being robbed by the world. However, Bruegel's world view is not all bleak in this painting. What can you see that shows peace and harmony?*

The Misanthrope, 1568

The Magpie on the Gallows, 1568

The Magpie, Claude Monet, 1869

Death

Bruegel died in 1569, a year after war had broken out. No one knows what caused his death but he died very young, in his mid-forties. Just before Bruegel died it is believed that he requested his wife to burn a series of captioned drawings, afraid that she might get into trouble if they were found once he had gone. This suggests that they may have been critical of the Spanish rulers, and had they been discovered his wife could have been imprisoned or sentenced to death.

Monet's magpie

Claude Monet's *The Magpie* was painted 300 years after Bruegel's death and can be interpreted as a tribute to him. Monet (1840–1926) has transformed Bruegel's gallows into a wooden gate, with the magpie on top. It is a cold scene with little life, but there is sunlight illuminating the snow, perhaps acknowledging Bruegel's legacy as an early master of winter landscapes.

Sons and heirs

Bruegel's fame and influence as a painter took off not long after his death. This led to great demand for his paintings, with many artists, including his sons, making copies of his work. His works have inspired artists to continue looking at the world in all its detail, from the wide vistas of nature, to the everyday lives of ordinary people.

Open Air Wedding Dance,
Pieter Brueghel the Younger, 1610

Flowers in a Wooden Vessel,
Jan Brueghel the Elder, 1607

Sons

Bruegel's sons were too young to have known their father when he died, but were inspired to follow in his footsteps. Pieter Brueghel the Younger (1564–1637/8) and Jan Brueghel the Elder (1568–1625) made many copies of their father's paintings and imitated his style. *Open Air Wedding Dance* by Pieter Brueghel the Younger is a version of his father's *The Wedding Dance* (see p.39). However they were also known for painting their own subjects.

Velvet Brueghel

Jan the Elder was considered the best painter of flowers of his day and earned the nickname "Velvet Brueghel" for his skill in representing delicate textures. Jan had two sons (Ambroisius and Jan the Younger) and a grandson (Abraham), all of whom also became painters.

Hell Brueghel

Pieter the Younger received the nickname "Hell Brueghel" as he made many paintings showing Hell and demons, much like his father's painting of *Dulle Griet* (see p.22).

Flatford Mill, John Constable, 1817

Lasting legacy

Bruegel's legacy can be seen in political cartoons, surrealist imagery and visual puzzles. He made scenes of man and nature that had a big influence on art and can be seen in works by artists such as the 19th century British painter John Constable.

"To Pieter Bruegel, flawless painter of most elegant skill, whom Nature herself, mother of all things, could well praise, whom the most experienced artists admire, and whose rivals imitate in vain."
– Tribute inscribed on Bruegel's headstone over a hundred years after his death.

Pottery about Bruegel

Like Bruegel, British artist Grayson Perry (1960–) is interested in showing the lives of ordinary people.

His urn *Punters in the Snow* is an updated image of Bruegel's *Hunters in the Snow*. It shows how lifestyles have changed from people living off the land for survival, to people going shopping for designer goods.

Punters in the Snow, Grayson Perry, 1999

Timeline

c.1523–1530   Pieter Bruegel is born, either in the town of Breda or Bree in the Netherlands

1545   is thought to study under the artist Pieter Coecke van Aelst, in Brussels

1551   registers his profession as a painter with the Antwerp Painter's Guild

travels to Italy, passing across the Swiss Alps

while in Italy, works alongside the painter Guilio Clovio in Rome

1553   returns to Antwerp, the Netherlands, and works on series of drawings called *Large Landscapes*

1555   begins working for the printing house of Hieronymus Cock

1556   draws *Big Fish Eat Little Fish*

completes series of print designs called *The Vices*

1557   paints *Landscape with the Parable of the Sower*

c.1558   paints *The Fall of Icarus*

1559   begins to sign his name "Bruegel" instead of "Brueghel"

paints *Netherlandish Proverbs*

1560   complete series of print designs *The Virtues*

paints *Children's Games*

1562   paints *Dulle Grieg (Mad Meg)*

paints *The Fall of the Rebel Angels*

paints *Triumph of Death*

leaves Antwerp to go to Amsterdam

1563   moves to Brussels and marries van Aelst's daughter

completes the print designs *The Fat Kitchen* and *The Lean Kitchen*

paints *Landscape with Flight into Egypt*

paints a version of the *Tower of Babel*

1564   eldest son, Pieter the Younger, is born

paints another version of the *Tower of Babel*

1565   paints the *Months*, a series of six paintings

paints *Winter Landscape with a Birdtrap*

1566   paints *The Wedding Dance*

draws *The Painter and the Art Lover*

1567   youngest son, Jan the Elder, is born

paints *Massacre of the Innocents*

paints the *Peasant Dance*

paints *Peasant Wedding*

Spanish king Philip II sends his army into the Netherlands to control Protestant rebellion

1568   paints *The Peasant and the Bird-nester*

draws *The Beekeepers*

paints *The Misanthrope*

paints *The Magpie on the Gallows*

start of the Eighty Year War between Spain and the Netherlands

1569   Bruegel dies and is buried in Notre Dame de la Chapelle in Brussels

selected works

The Procession to Calvary, 1564 (p.7)

This is one of largest pictures Bruegel ever painted and it is teeming with detail. It shows the scene of Jesus carrying a large cross to Calvary, the place where he is to be crucified (top right). Although Jesus is in the very center of the composition, he is hard to discover on first sight, dwarfed by the activity of the crowds and the larger figures in the foreground. These figures are the Virgin Mary and her companions, all grief-stricken at what is taking place behind them. Only they and Jesus are dressed in clothes worn at the time of the crucifixion; everyone else is wearing outfits from Bruegel's time. The landscape and windmill also transport the event to 16th century Netherlands, which has led some experts to view the painting as a comment on the politics and beliefs of this time, with most of the crowd showing a large indifference to the fate of Jesus, acting as a parallel to their Netherlandish future.

Haymaking, 1565 (p.30)

This painting represents the early summer months of June and July and is filled with pale green colors common to the plant life at this time of year. It shows people making hay and gathering fruit and vegetables. A sense of depth is created by the diagonal line that begins on the bottom left following the path (which features a shrine to the Virgin Mary), along a series of sloping fields towards the meandering river that disappears into the horizon.

The Gloomy Day, 1565 (p.28)

This painting is the darkest of the *Months*, and is dominated by earthy colors. An exception is the contrasting cleaner whites, blues and reds of the figures in the foreground, and the white of the house on the right counterbalanced by the snow-covered mountains towards the top left. The harsh, gloomy weather of February is shown in the dark colors, the heavy clouds and the high waves rocking the boats out at sea. It is the season when the leafless trees are lopped for firewood, an activity that is taking place in the painting. The trees form a central column, dividing the image between the receding landscape to the left and the figures on the right. Not all the figures are working however. Some are eating waffles and wearing a paper crown, traditional customs for carnival which occurred in February, before Lent.

Peasant Wedding, 1567 (p.36)

In *Peasant Wedding* the identity of the bride is made clear by decorative customs of the time. She is seated in front of a sheet of material known as a "cloth of honor" and under a paper crown, both marking her out as important to the day's event. However, where is the groom? He may be one of several figures around the table, he may be serving the food, or he may even be in the position of the viewer. The three men at the right of the table stand out from the rest of the group in the clothes that they are wearing. The man in the hood is a friar, whereas the man to his left is a judge: he wears a fur-trimmed jacket and is given the honor of sitting in a chair. The man at the very end has a sword and is the most smartly and wealthily dressed in the room; he is likely to be a landowner.

The Magpie on the Gallows, 1568 (p.41)

This painting is framed on either side by trees, with the wooden gallows standing in the very center. Human life occupies the left of the image, whereas on the right side of the gallows the painting is largely empty of people and filled with a cross marking a grave and the skull of an animal in the foreground. The people dancing represent the Dutch proverb: "to dance under the gallows," meaning to tempt fate. It is possible that this is a comment on careless behavior leading to death, with symbols of death (the grave and skull) appearing opposite the peasants.

Glossary

accurate when something is correct, such as a truthful representation in art

apprentice a person who is learning a new skill or job by working for an expert in that profession

caricature representation of a person for comic effect, by exaggerating parts of their body, behavior or facial features

censorship the editing or removal of information or artwork that might threaten the reputation or rule of a person or government

civilized an educated and well-mannered person and/or the state of a society with an advanced and well-developed culture and government

commission where a person or an organization asks an artist to produce work in return for paying a fee

composition how all the elements of an image, such as a painting, fit together

customs an established way of behaving or a belief that has existed for a long time, such as a ritual that has formed part of a country's tradition

depiction a representation of something made in a drawing or painting

dispute a disagreement or argument

elements things that make up the natural environment, including earth, air and water

engraver a person who cuts lines into a metal plate often copying images based on drawings, the metal plate is then used to make a print

engraving a picture printed onto paper from a piece of wood or metal into which a design has been cut

exaggerate to represent something as larger, bigger, more important, better or worse than it really is

extinction the disappearance or destruction of a species from the Earth

fantastical something that is unusual and remarkable, strange and imaginary

flawless perfect and without mistakes

foreground the part of an image that appears closest to the viewer

fortitude courage and strength in the face of difficulty

gallows a structure usually built from two upright beams attached by one crosspiece from which criminals are hanged

genre painting painting of realistic scenes that show the everyday life of ordinary people at work or at play

glaze a thin covering with a smooth and shiny surface

gluttony the habit of eating and drinking too much

grotesque something that looks very ugly, almost unnatural and sometimes comical

harmony different elements working well together

ideal something that is perfect or exists in the imagination as perfect, but may not exist in real life

illuminated manuscript a handwritten book with images that decorate parts of pages, such as the margins, and sometimes includes full-page miniature paintings

imagery pictures and descriptive language that often fire the imagination

imitate to copy the work or behavior of someone, or behave in a similar way

impasto the process of applying paint thickly

legacy something that is handed down from the past, from someone that has died or from an event in history. This can be a collection of work, money, a style or a way of thinking

legend a popular story from the past that is not always true

light box a flat box that contains a light that lights up the top surface; often used by photographers to examine photographic transparencies and negatives

massacre the cruel killing of many people

medieval a period in history, also known as the Middle Ages, that covers the 5th to the 15th century

miniaturist person who paints small-scale paintings, such as illustrated manuscripts

misanthrope someone who dislikes people

monumental something that is very big, resembling a monument or statue; something that has outstanding significance

moral concerned with judgements of what is considered right or wrong in the way someone behaves and acts

mounted placed on top of

mourning the actions and expressions of sorrow after someone's death. In some countries this is shown by wearing black clothes

myth a traditional story, sometimes from ancient history, that often contains magical occurrences or events

palette a range of colors used by an artist

parchment the skin of a goat or sheep that has been prepared for use as a writing surface or high quality paper that has been made to resemble this

patron a person who buys works of art or supports an artist or a cause

peasant a person who earns a small wage working in the countryside, such as a farm worker

pose the deliberate positioning of the person's body for a painting or drawing

Protestant Reformation a religious movement in the 16th century that began as an attempt to reform the Catholic Church and resulted in the creation of Protestant Churches

proverb a saying that contains a commonly believed truth or piece of advice

province a part of a country, sometimes existing as an independent region

prudence the quality of being careful, showing good judgement and common sense

pulleys a set of grooved wheels over which ropes or chains pass, supporting the lifting or lowering of heavy objects

Renaissance a period in history, around the mid-14th to late 16th century, where the learning and culture of ancient Greece and Rome were revived

Roman Catholic Church the largest branch of Christianity, of which the Pope is the head

sanitation conditions that affect your health; keeping things clean such as removing sewage and dirt

satire use of humour to comment on social and political issues

scholar a person who studies a subject in great detail, such as a student at university

sinister to give the impression of something evil

sloth an unwillingness to work or make an effort; laziness

surreal showing something dreamlike and unfamiliar; having come from the unconscious mind or from a dream

Surrealism an artistic movement from the twentieth century that looked to express the creativity of the unconscious mind

symbol an object used to represent something which cannot be seen, such as an idea or feeling

technicolor the description of something that has bright, vivid colors

temperance self-control

traditional a way of doing something, behaving and thinking that has been in use for a long time

tragic describes a sad and serious event; the opposite of something that is comic

translucent a surface that is clear enough to allow light to pass through it

treadwheel crane a crane used for lifting and lowering large objects, powered by humans walking inside a giant wheel

tribute an act or a gift that shows appreciation and admiration for someone or something

uncanny something that is strange and mysterious in an unsettling way

unconscious part of the mind that is not awake and aware of the world, but can influence feelings and behavior

vice an immoral habit or action

vista a distant view

winches lifting devices powered by turning a handle or wheel that is connected to ropes or chains

world landscape a style of painting that attempts to capture as much of the world's scenery within its frame, shown from a high viewpoint

For More Information

Books

Harvey, Damian. *Pieter Bruegel the Elder.* London, England: Franklin Watts, 2014.

Sellink, Manfred. *Bruegel in Detail.* New York, NY: Abrams, 2014.

Shafer, Anders C. *The Fantastic Journey of Pieter Bruegel.* New York, NY: Dutton Children's Books, 2002.

Websites

Because of the changing nature of Internet links, Rosen Publishing has developed an online list of websites related to the subject of this book. This site is updated regularly. Please use this link to access this list:

http://www.rosenlinks.com/ART/Bru

Index